AUSTRALIA IN HIST

# Australia
## *and the*
# Second World War,
# 1939-45

A.K. Macdougall

Waverton Press

Waverton Press
Level 1
100 Bay Road
Waverton NSW 2060
Australia
Email: publishing@fivemile.com.au

First published 2004

Edited by Samone Bos
Designed by Sylvia Witte

Printed in China

National Library of Australia Cataloguing-in-Publication data
Macdougall, A. K. (Anthony Keith), 1943– .
Australia and the Second World War.

Includes index.
For lower to middle secondary students.
ISBN 1 74124 090 5.

1. World War, 1939–1945 – Australia – Juvenile literature.
I. Title.  (Series: Australia in history).

940.5394

The photographs in this book came mostly from the author's
collection.

The following photographs are reproduced courtesy of the
Australian War Memorial, Canberra: Page 7 (top) (AWM photo
9211); page 7 (lower) (AWM photo 439); page 11; page 12 (AWM
photo 2110); page 13 (AWM photo 6400); page 15 (AWM photo
6387); page 17 (AWM photo 10305); page 18 and cover (top left)
(AWM photo 10980); page 24 (AWM photo 151392); page 25
(AWM photo 9153/25); page 26 (AWM photo 30532/13); page
27; page 31 (AWM photo 18008). Cover photograph (top right)
of Australian soldier in slouch hat: (AWM photo 17342).

The painting on page 23 and the photographs on pages 28 and
30 are from United States official sources (National Archives,
Washington).

Every attempt has been made to trace and acknowledge
copyright. Where an attempt has been unsuccessful, the
publisher would be pleased to hear from the copyright owner so
any omission or error can be rectified.

# ontents

# 1933-39:
## The march to war

**A**fter the signing of the Treaty of Versailles in 1919, it was hoped that Europe would have a future free of wars. During the 1920s, the **Great Powers** carried out a program of **disarmament**, limiting naval strength by the Washington Naval Treaty (1922). Much reliance was placed on the League of Nations to avert further conflicts, which convened at Geneva, Switzerland, in 1920.

The 1920s became a bright, free-spending period that ended suddenly with the Wall Street stock market crash of 1929. By 1930 an economic **recession** began to engulf the world. People's confidence in their societies was shattered.

## The Depression

The 'Depression' – known in Britain as the 'Slump' – caused factory shut-downs, a collapse of trade, widespread unemployment and enormous social distress. Many in the world saw democracy as a failure and looked to political alternatives. Some pointed to the seeming success of **dictatorships** such as the first Fascist State, Italy, which Benito Mussolini (1883–1945) had ruled since 1922.

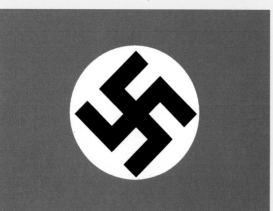

*Nazi Germany's flag bearing the 'hooked cross' – or swastika – soon became feared throughout Europe.*

## Dictatorships

Mussolini's counterpart soon arose in Germany. Adolf Hitler (1889–1945) was an Austrian-born ex-soldier who had long been viewed as a harmless, slightly mad rabble-rouser during the 1920s. Hitler was a peculiar, obsessive man and led a small political party called the National Socialist German Workers' Party – known widely as the 'Nazis' – whose banner bore the ancient symbol of the swastika ('hooked cross'). He traced his country's ills to the **Communists**, the 'Jewish financiers' and the Treaty of Versailles, which after the First World War had left Germany's army so weak that it was almost defenceless.

The National Socialists appealed to social misfits, workers and patriotic Germans alike, though its brutish tactics appalled many. As unemployment rose in Germany, Hitler's Nazi Party gained the support of industrialists because Hitler promised to restore Germany's productivity and prosperity and suppress Communism (Bolshevism).

Most Germans rejected the Nazis – when Hitler stood for president in 1932 he received only 37 per cent of the vote. But during 1932 democracy was failing in Germany: there were five elections in that year alone, with no party achieving a clear majority. Even in the **Reichstag** elections, where dozens died in fighting between Nazis and Communists, the Nazis again only won 37 per cent of the seats. However, in January 1933, Hitler was invited by President Hindenburg to head a **coalition** government in Germany, if only to defuse Nazi violence. Only three of the 11 cabinet ministers were Nazis, and it was hoped that the other parties could keep the Nazis in check. It was a fatal

miscalculation – one of the new Nazi ministers, Goering, as Minister for Prussia, had control of two-thirds of the German police.

Within weeks, the Nazis had driven well-known Communists and Socialists into prison or hiding. Hitler demanded and obtained total power from the divided parties in the Reichstag and promptly threw his opponents into 'concentration camps'. Anti-Jewish laws followed. The Nazi party soon controlled German newspapers, broadcasting and films. Hitler's **propaganda** minister, Goebbels, dictated his peoples' thinking. Germany and Europe had entered a new dark age.

## ... And the drift to war

In 1935, Hitler – Germany's new 'Fuehrer' (leader) – announced the formation of an air force (*Luftwaffe*) and reintroduced **conscription** – two acts that broke the Treaty of Versailles. He began building the most modern and powerful army in Europe, and Britain and France also began to rearm. Mussolini's Italy invaded Ethiopia (Abyssinia), and the League of Nations expelled Italy for aggression, calling for sanctions that proved ineffective. Early in 1936, Hitler sent troops into the demilitarised region between France and Germany, the Rhineland, and signed a friendship pact with Italy.

Britain and France, fearful of war, did nothing over the Rhineland, and decided to 'appease' Hitler. France's strong web of alliances with Poland, Czechoslovakia, Romania and Yugoslavia began to unravel. Four months later, the Spanish Army under General Franco rose up against Spain's Socialist republic, and both Germany and Italy sent forces to Franco's aid. In 1937, Japan – already expelled from the League of Nations for invading Manchuria in 1931 – attacked China, while the world again stood by, powerless to act.

In March 1938, Hitler marched his armies into Austria, bringing it into the **Reich**. In September, he demanded the return of another German-speaking region – the Sudetenland, in the Republic of Czechoslovakia. When the Czechs mobilised for war, Britain's Prime Minister Neville Chamberlain negotiated an agreement with Hitler. By the shameful Munich Agreement,

Czechoslovakia was forced to hand over to Hitler the Sudetenland, which contained the Czech frontier fortresses, leaving the nation defenceless.

In 1936, Hitler (right) and Italy's Mussolini (left) proclaimed their policy of making the 'Berlin-Rome Axis' the new power in Europe.

# 1939 : War declared

After his bloodless victory at Munich, Hitler was triumphant and proclaimed that he had 'no further territorial claims in Europe'. But in mid-March 1939, Hitler encouraged the Slovaks to proclaim their independence and the next day marched his forces into Prague to 'protect' the Czechs. He was now revealed as a leader whose promises could never be trusted. In April 1939 – when Mussolini invaded Albania – Britain and France, realizing that only force could now stop Hitler, promised Poland, Greece and Romania that they would aid them if Germany attacked them.

In search of an ally, Britain now looked to the Soviet Union, which, under Stalin, had become a dictatorship dwarfing even Hitler's Germany in size and its ruthless use of terror. But Hitler moved first. On 23 August 1939, Germany and Stalin's Soviet Union signed a treaty of friendship. By a secret clause, the dictators agreed to divide Poland, a nation they both found intolerable.

At dawn on 1 September 1939, German forces attacked Poland without warning. Everyone wondered if Britain and France would again give way to Hitler. Poland crumbled under attacks by German tanks and bombers. But at 11 a.m. on Sunday 3 September, the British Prime Minister, Neville Chamberlain, announced over the wireless that Hitler had refused to withdraw his forces from Poland, and that 'as a result, this country is at war with Germany'.

## Australia goes to war

There were no cheering crowds when the announcement was made. Even in Berlin the people were silent, as if in shock. When Britain declared war on Germany, she had no allies. Her empire was strong but her 'self-governing **Dominions**' were now independent nations with no obligation to join Britain in any war. But only half an hour after Mr Chamberlain's speech was broadcast to Australia, the Australian Prime Minister, Robert Menzies, announced on the radio that 'as a result, Australia is also at war'. New Zealand followed within hours.

The two distant Dominions were the first nations to pledge support to Britain in its struggle with Nazi Germany. France declared war on Germany just five hours later. South Africa declared war on Germany on 6 September and Canada entered on 10 September. The Viceroy of India committed India to war alongside Britain. The United States immediately declared **neutrality**, and so did Italy.

None of these nations at war thought that this conflict would soon become a 'Second World War' – one even more terrible than the First World War. Soon the world was to see the beginning of six years of horror that would cause the deaths of 55 million people in Europe and Asia.

A wartime poster shows the men of the British Empire marching to war. From top (clockwise) are shown servicemen from Africa, India, New Zealand, Britain, Australia, Canada and South Africa.

In population, the foes were evenly matched. Both Britain and France each had 40 million people; Germany 80 million. Australia, with a population of seven million, and New Zealand with fewer than two million, seemed unlikely to play any significant role in the war. Yet the armed forces they raised, small in number, were to fight on every battlefront: from the deserts of the Middle East to the jungles of the Pacific; their warships would serve from the Arctic Circle to the Pacific, their airmen see action from Norway to Burma.

## The 'phoney war'

In London and Paris, people waited for German aircraft to rain bombs and poison gas on them, but no attacks came and people breathed freely again. The British Army's five divisions took their place along the Belgian frontier on the left of the 130 divisions of the French Army, just as they had done in the First World War in 1914. The powerful French Army waited in its strong line of fortifications on the German frontier – the Maginot Line – but for eight months nothing happened. An American politician called the war a 'phoney war'. No military offensives or air raids were mounted, apart from British planes dropping propaganda leaflets imploring the German people to rise up against Hitler.

## Australian forces

As they had done in 1914, the Dominions called on volunteers to serve overseas in an army for the British Empire's defence – the Second AIF. In Australia, which had five army divisions of militia for home defence, 20,000 volunteers were formed into a 'Special Force' for overseas service, soon named the 6th Division and placed under the command of Major-General Sir Thomas Blamey. Many young men volunteered for the air force, joining the 'Empire Air Training Scheme' (EATS), to train here and in Canada as pilots, navigators, engineers and gunners.

The Royal Australian Navy sent its entire destroyer flotilla to the Mediterranean to assist the British – they were soon joined by four of the five modern cruisers.

Britain mobilised its entire people during 1940–41, but in Australia the war was remote until the Japanese attack. In 1941, Australian women were able to volunteer in their own army, naval and air corps; and not until 1942 was rationing of food and petrol introduced.

Above: As the Allied situation worsened, Australian women began joining the armed forces. This photograph shows personnel of the Women's Royal Australian Navy Service (WRANS).

Left: An army of Australian volunteers sailed for war in early 1940. They were destined to fight in the Middle East for two years.

# 1939: Poland and war in the north

## Poland defeated

**P**oland was crushed in just four weeks. The *Luftwaffe* bombed Warsaw, and German armies struck ruthlessly from north, west and south. Polish cavalry charges against tanks were heroic but useless.

Russia's armies entering Poland on 17 September 1939 dealt the death-blow to the Poles, and eastern Poland passed under Soviet rule. Despite a brave defence, Warsaw and Poland's armies were forced to surrender in October. Soon, Poland's large Jewish population was herded into 'ghettos' in the big cities, where they were half-starved and began to die. Under German rule nearly six million Poles were to perish. 'We are the Master Race,' a Nazi Gauleiter in Poland informed his officials. The Slav people would be reduced to slavery. The hideous nature of Nazi rule was revealed early.

## Finland

The dictators now threatened the peaceful states of Scandinavia. Stalin, who never completely trusted Hitler, decided to remove threats from his borders. In December 1939, Soviet armies invaded Finland. They advanced in the snows of winter and the skilled Finnish ski-troops quickly

*Germany's army in 1939 was the most modern in Europe.*

devised tactics to defeat them – by attacking their columns, isolating the Russians.

For three months, the world watched with admiration as the Finns, under their commander, Marshal Mannerheim, fought back the Russians, who suffered 200,000 casualties. But by March 1940, as Allied leaders were discussing a hare-brained scheme to send an army of 100,000 through Norway to aid the Finns, a reinforced Russian Army broke through the Mannerheim Line defending Helsinki and forced the Finns to sign an **armistice**.

## Russia seizes the Baltic states

After defeating Finland, in March 1940 Stalin then marched into the three Baltic states that had won their independence from Russia in 1919 – Latvia, Lithuania and Estonia. He annexed them and then demanded the return of Romania's northern border region of Bessarabia.

## Denmark and Norway

The northern Norwegian port of Narvik, from where Swedish iron ore was shipped to Germany, had long been of interest to both the British and Germans. To safeguard the port, in February 1940 Hitler made plans to invade Norway, while Britain's Navy planned to mine Norway's territorial waters.

Early on 9 April 1940, Germany seized the small kingdom of Denmark without resistance and landed forces along Norway's coast. Despite the treachery of the Norwegian Colonel Quisling – his name became a byword for traitor – the Norwegians fought back; their forts at Oslo sank several German warships, and their forces were assisted by an Anglo-French force which landed near the northern ports of Narvik and Namsos. But the Allied troops were ill-equipped, and the British at one stage had only 20 aircraft to fight nearly 1,000 German planes. They fought for nearly two months before being evacuated.

The British Navy sank most of the German warships in two spirited attacks in Narvik, but the campaign was soon aborted. At sea, where Britain's Navy was powerful, several German ships were hunted down, and a maritime blockade began. It was hoped that the blockade would, in time, weaken Germany.

## Weapons of war

The Allies expected the war to be a repeat of the 1914–18 conflict. They would avoid bloodshed by awaiting attack, not initiating it. They knew the destructive power of the machine-gun and placed extreme reliance in tanks. Both Germany and France had 2,500 tanks and the Allies felt confident of outlasting their enemy.

Germany's air force – the *Luftwaffe* – helped destroy Poland's defences and civilian populace.

# 1940:
# Blitzkrieg in the west

**O**n the morning of 10 May 1940, the very day that Winston Churchill became Britain's Prime Minister, Germany attacked the 'Low Countries' – Belgium, the Netherlands and Luxembourg. Their people had seen newsreel film of Germany's terrifying *blitzkrieg* – 'Lightning War' – on Poland, but they now experienced its full fury. Rotterdam was bombed and parachute troops captured Dutch bridges and strong-points before the Dutch could flood their flat and defenceless land to delay the invaders. On 15 May 1940, the Dutch surrendered.

As in 1914, the Germans attacked France through Belgium, choosing to send their tanks through the mountainous Ardennes, a terrain considered too difficult for tanks and only thinly defended. On 15 May 1940, German armoured divisions aided by strong air forces – including Stuka dive-bombers – emerged from the Ardennes forests and broke through the French front at Sedan, pouring like an 'expanding torrent' behind the French lines. On this day the battle of France was decided.

The Germans concentrated their tanks into 10 fast-moving 'Panzer' divisions. The French had spread their tanks and aircraft along the entire front, and possessed only three armoured divisions with which to strike back. German tanks were soon streaming behind the French armies, while aircraft bombed towns and fleeing French refugees.

*Right: Britain's Prime Minister Winston Churchill giving his famous 'V for Victory' sign after making a speech. Churchill pledged: 'We will never surrender' and led Britain and the Commonwealth through the hard years of the war.*

## Dunkirk: Saving the army

The entire British Army in northern France had rushed into Belgium to stop the Germans, and began a fighting retreat to the Channel port of Dunkirk, where they were soon surrounded. On 26 May 1940, Churchill ordered the navy to save the British force at Dunkirk. Two days later, the King of the Belgians ordered his army to surrender to the Germans.

Soon, from England's southern ports nearly a thousand small boats, steamers, yachts, fishing smacks, ferries and motorboats headed for the beaches of Dunkirk to save the army. In four days, they and the Royal Navy brought back to England 330,000 soldiers, one-third of them French. It was a stirring moment and showed the world that the British people would not give up easily.

## The fall of France

Meanwhile, the French high command seemed paralysed. The Commander-in-Chief General Gamelin had lost contact with his armies and orders were issued and then countermanded, confusing his generals. Allied air forces had been shot from the sky. The French armies fell back to the River Somme, the scene of great battles in the First World War, but German armour broke through.

On 14 June 1940 the Nazis entered Paris.

Churchill begged France to fight on, but France's losses had been terrible – nearly 100,000 soldiers killed. Four days later, the new French Premier, the hero of Verdun, Marshal Pétain, asked Germany for an armistice. Half of France was occupied by the Germans, the other half ruled by Pétain's government which collaborated with Nazi Germany. A junior French general named Charles de Gaulle flew to England and appealed to the French to continue the war against Germany, but few joined him. No one had imagined that the great French Republic, which had withstood four years of bloodshed in the 1914–18 war, would collapse in just six weeks.

For exactly one year from that date – 22 June 1940 – Britain and her Commonwealth fought alone against Germany and its new ally Italy, sustained only by increasing aid from the United States. America's President Franklin D. Roosevelt did all he could – 'everything short of war' – to aid the British people with weapons and **munitions**.

As tens of thousands of men volunteered for service, the Australian government announced the formation of new divisions: soon the AIF consisted of the 6th, 7th, 8th and 9th Divisions and in August 1940 alone 100,000 men joined up.

## The Battle of Britain

Nearly 500 Australian airmen were in Britain serving with the Royal Air Force (RAF) in 1939, and they fought in all the campaigns from Norway to France. Their fighter pilots were soon to fight in 'The Battle of Britain'. With France now removed from the war, Hitler appealed to Britain for peace. The British rejected his offer and Churchill vowed to fight on 'until every last vestige of Nazism is destroyed'. In late July 1940, as Hitler gathered barges and landing craft to invade England, the German air offensive against Britain began, aiming to destroy the RAF as a prelude to invasion.

Britain had only 500 fighter aircraft left, but they were among the fastest, best-armed fighters in the world – Hurricanes and Spitfires, capable of speeds exceeding 550 kilometres per hour. The British also had 'radar' which showed approaching enemy aircraft as blips on a cathode screen. In mid-August 1940, the Germans attacked English airfields with 1,400 aircraft (bomber and fighter escorts) but the faster Hurricanes and Spitfires fought back superbly.

In three weeks, the Germans lost 450 aircraft, and by mid-September had lost a total of 800 aircraft while the British had lost 400 pilots. Hitler cancelled invasion plans and the *Luftwaffe* moved their attacks to London itself, bombing civilian areas. 'The Blitz' lasted until May 1941 and killed 40,000 British civilians but failed to break Britain's resolve. Of the pilots in Britain's Fighter Command, Churchill said: 'Never in the field of human conflict was so much owed by so many to so few.'

Wartime poster paying tribute to the fighter-pilots of the RAF after the Battle of Britain.

# 1940: The Mediterranean

## War against Italy

On 10 June 1940, Mussolini, who seemed sure that the war was soon to end in a German victory, took Italy into the war on Germany's side. Mussolini was eager to share in the spoils of victory, but his armed forces were weak and his generals advised that Italy would not be ready for war until 1942. The Italian people – traditionally anti-German and friendly to Britain – were weary of the Fascist regime.

## The war at sea

The Mediterranean then became a war front, and for two years it remained the major British battlefront. The British Mediterranean Fleet under Admiral Sir Andrew Cunningham, though outnumbered, sought to entice Italy's modern and powerful fleet to do battle. The old Australian destroyers commanded by Commander 'Hec' Waller were soon joined by the Australian cruiser HMAS *Sydney* and fought in the first engagements. Only a month after the outbreak of war with Italy, *Sydney*, under Captain John Collins, tackled two Italian cruisers off western Crete (July 1940) and sank one of them, the *Bartolomeo Colleoni*, and damaged the other. She had repeated the spectacular action of her predecessor, the first HMAS *Sydney*, and became a national icon.

Britain's great asset was her aircraft carriers, which enabled her fleet to seek out their enemy. On Remembrance Day (11 November) 1940, Cunningham launched torpedo-carrying aircraft from HMS *Illustrious* in a surprise night-attack on the Italians in Taranto Harbour and sank three battleships.

## Rome~Berlin~Tokyo Axis, 1940

In September 1940, Germany, Italy and Japan signed the Tri-partite Alliance in Berlin, pledging to create a 'New Order' in the world. That month German forces moved into Romania, previously an ally of France and Britain, but now without allies. Romanian oil would fuel Hitler's war machine for the next four years.

The Axis alliance showed that Japan had decided to pursue her successful program of aggression, but Britain still hoped Japan would remain neutral. After the fall of France, Japan had demanded rights to base forces in French Indo-China. This move greatly concerned Australia because it brought Japan dangerously close.

Australian troops arriving in the Middle East in 1940 were put through hard training for the desert war.

## Italy defeated in Greece and Libya

Mussolini was already regretting entering the war with little to show, and decided to build a new empire in the Balkans. On 28 October 1940, his army in Albania attacked Greece. The Italian armies, woefully ill-equipped, were pushed back by strong Greek resistance, and spent the cold winter **stalemated** in the snows.

Mussolini had also counted on a quick Italian conquest of Egypt by his armies in Libya, because his forces there numbered 250,000 men and in Abyssinia (Ethiopia) were another 200,000. General Wavell's British Middle East command based in Egypt could muster only 60,000 men, even after being slowly reinforced by British Empire troops. By early 1941, two Australian divisions had reached Egypt (the 6th and 7th Divisions) along with the New Zealand Division, and the 4th Indian Division. Soon, tough Anzac infantry would be in the thick of the fighting.

The Italian armies had moved forward in September in the last heat of summer, and were inside the Egyptian frontier, but were greatly extended and far from their main base of Tripoli. In December 1940, the British and Indians attacked the Italians suddenly and broke them. The British 7th Armoured Division (known as the 'Desert Rats') crossed the desert to encircle an oncoming Italian tank force, and left the capture of the coastal towns of Bardia and Tobruk to the 6th Australian Division. Both seaports were strong fortresses, ringed with wire and anti-tank ditches.

## Bardia and Tobruk

In their first land-battle of the war, the Australians attacked Bardia on the morning of 3 January 1941, assisted by 18 British tanks. They captured it after a three-day battle, taking 40,000 prisoners for the loss of 456 Australians killed or wounded. Advancing without rest, the Australians then attacked Tobruk (21 January) and captured it in two days, taking 25,000 prisoners for the loss of 355 men. Two weeks later, the Australians entered Benghazi. They had been part of the most rapid victory in military history. The British force had advanced 700 kilometres, taking a total of 130,000 prisoners, and eagerly awaited orders to press on to Tripoli and eliminate Mussolini's north African empire. It was not to be.

General Wavell was ordered to send his desert army to help Greece. In March 1941, as the troops were landing in Greece, leaving the desert front almost undefended, the German-Italian Army under a new general, Erwin Rommel, attacked. The British retreated, leaving the 9th Australian Division in Tobruk, which they were ordered to defend for 'at least eight weeks'. The Australians were to defend Tobruk for eight months.

**The famous Australian cruiser HMAS Sydney saw intense action in the war against Italy, alongside the RAN destroyers of the 'Scrap Iron Flotilla'.**

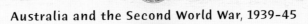

# 1941: The Balkans, Greece and Crete

In 1941, the Balkans became the focus of world attention. The Anzac forces were destined again to play a dramatic part in a desperate Balkan campaign. In February 1941, Hitler announced to his generals his decision to invade Russia in mid-May and finally remove the threat posed by the giant Communist power. To secure a southern flank, deprive the Allies of a base at Salonika and protect his Romanian oilfields, Hitler would take northern Greece.

In February 1941, Churchill sent his foreign minister Anthony Eden to convince the Balkan nations to unite against Hitler. With the armies of Turkey, Greece, Yugoslavia and Bulgaria, Britain could form a strong Balkan front. Churchill resolved to send an army to Greece's assistance, but the only troops available were the 6th Australian Division and the New Zealanders, accompanied by a brigade of 100 British tanks. General Blamey was worried that the entire Anzac Army was being sent to Greece, where it could be lost.

British plans were soon thrown into disarray. On 1 March 1941, Hitler forced Bulgaria to join the Axis and allow the entry of German forces. On 24 March, Hitler threatened Hungary with destruction unless it joined the Axis, and one day later he forced Yugoslavia to join. Greece's borders were now almost defenceless.

But on 27 March 1941, Serbian officers mounted a *coup d'état* in Belgrade, toppling the pro-Axis government and declaring neutrality. Churchill rejoiced at the Serbs' bravery, but Hitler was furious, and ordered Yugoslavia 'destroyed' and Greece invaded at the same time. He would

**Hitler bullied Hungary, Bulgaria and Yugoslavia into joining the Axis Pact in 1941. Soon after Prince Paul of Yugoslavia visited Hitler, Serb officers in Belgrade overthrew his government and proclaimed neutrality. Hitler invaded Yugoslavia and Greece regardless.**

use 13 divisions and a *Luftflotte* of 1000 aircraft. Only the weary Greek Army and two Anzac divisions faced him, supported by 80 British aircraft. Because of the Balkan mess, Hitler postponed his invasion of Russia from 15 May to 22 June – a fateful decision.

## Greece and Yugoslavia

The German invasion of Yugoslavia and Greece began on 6 April 1941. German armoured forces drove through the country with ease, suffering barely 100 dead and taking Yugoslavia's surrender 10 days later. Yugoslavia ceased to exist. It was split up into an independent Croatia, and the rest was occupied by Germany, Italy, Bulgaria, Hungary and Romania. Thousands of Yugoslav soldiers retreated into the mountains – the future royalist Chetniks who with Tito's Communist partisans would grow into a formidable resistance army.

## The Greek campaign

When the German tanks entered northern Greece, the 6th Australian Division and the New Zealanders near Mount Olympus were forced to retreat south, detonating the roads and bridges behind them. The over-pressed Greek armies collapsed under German air and tank attack and most of the British tanks were destroyed in one skirmish. On 12 April 1941, General Blamey informed his men that they were now 'Anzac Corps', and reminded them that their predicament was 'difficult but not nearly so desperate' as that faced by the Anzacs 26 years before. Nine days later, Wavell issued orders that the Anzacs were to be evacuated.

On 24 April 1941, as the Greek armies surrendered, the Anzac force drove through Athens with the Greek people still cheering them. The Anzacs were to be taken off the beaches of Attica and southern Greece by the navy. Of the 64,000 British and Empire soldiers in Greece, 14,000 were lost. The Germans entered Athens and raised the swastika flag over the Acropolis two days later.

**Italian prisoners in jubilant Greek hands, December 1940.**

## The battle for Crete

Many of the British and Anzac forces had been landed in Crete where one of the most bitter battles of the war was soon fought. On 25 April 1941, Hitler ordered that Crete be captured by airborne troops and that the battle must be resolved in seven days. He would hurl against Crete his paratroops and glider-borne infantry. Commanded by the New Zealander, Major-General Bernard Freyberg, VC, the 15,000 Australian and New Zealand infantry and 15,000 ill-equipped British troops had no aircraft left, but they had the support of the Cretan people, who resolved to die fighting by their side.

On 20 May 1941, the German airborne invasion began. The blue sky was thick with German aircraft, gliders and blossoming parachutes and the defenders fought back ruthlessly. Within a day, the Germans had secured an airfield. On 27 May, after a week of desperate fighting in the heat, the defenders were ordered to retreat to the south coast to be evacuated. Some Australian battalions defending Retimo airstrip fought on until they were surrounded. The fleet came in night after night to lift the exhausted troops, but 4,000 Australians and 5,000 New Zealanders were left behind on Crete – killed, wounded and prisoners. Caught in the daylight by the *Luftwaffe*, the Royal Navy lost three cruisers and six destroyers sunk, two battleships and a carrier damaged. This brave battle was another crushing defeat. Australia's Prime Minister Menzies, visiting London, was appalled to learn that two Australians divisions had nearly been lost, for the 9th Division was now surrounded in Tobruk.

# *1941*: The Middle East: Small victories

## Tobruk

In April 1941, Rommel's advancing Nazi Afrika Korps reached Tobruk and attacked its defences. They were thrown back by a torrent of gunfire from the 9th Australian Division. It was the beginning of a mighty siege that became the first defeat suffered by the German Army in two years of war. Under the command of Major-General Morshead, a strong leader, the Australians not only knocked back German and Italian attacks, but counter-attacked at night. As summer's heat wore on, the Australians suffered from lack of water and insufficient food, but the navy, including the five Australian destroyers, ferried in supplies at night and took out the wounded. Radio Berlin described the Australians as 'caught like rats in a trap' so the 9th Division called themselves the 'Rats of Tobruk'. Enemy radio insultingly called the old Australian destroyers a 'pile of scrap iron', so the Aussie sailors dubbed their ships the 'Scrap Iron Flotilla'.

## Iraq and Iran

As Greece crumbled and the desert front collapsed, Britain's position in the Middle East deteriorated further. Iraq, like Egypt, was nominally independent but had had to accept the presence of British bases in their territory. In March 1941, a nationalist leader named Rashid Ali seized the chance to expel the British with German aid, and mounted a coup in Baghdad. German assistance did not arrive. British troops promptly landed at Basra (as they had done in 1914, and were to do again in 2003), and a column of armoured cars struck across the desert from Transjordan and quickly crushed the revolt with almost no bloodshed. Iraq was occupied peacefully by the British until the end of the war. In August 1941, British troops in Iraq marched into Iran to secure the country, occupying it until 1945.

## Syria

Churchill was alarmed to hear that German aircraft were flying from Greece to Syria, which remained under the authority of the pro-German Vichy French government. The leader of Free France, General de Gaulle, was determined to bring Syria under his control, but Syria was defended by 40,000 Vichy French troops. The only strong force Wavell could muster was the 7th Australian Division

**Right: The arrival of the German general Erwin Rommel (left) and the powerful tank units of the 'Afrika Korps' transformed the desert war. But Rommel was unable to break the Australian defence of Tobruk.**

**Right:** The men of the 9th Australian Division marooned in Tobruk dug deep defences and repulsed constant enemy attacks on the port.

– the so-far 'Silent Seventh' – which led the advance into Syria on 8 June 1941.

The Syrian campaign proved to be one of the hardest-fought campaigns of the war. The French on the coast resisted strongly. The mountainous terrain and narrow roads were strongly defended. The Australians, as in 1918, were the first into Damascus, which they entered on 21 June, and were approaching Beirut when the French C-in-C signed an armistice on 12 July. Fighting against a former ally had cost 1,600 Australian casualties. Australia's No. 3 Squadron, RAAF, flew Tomahawk (P-40) fighters in the Syrian campaign: the unit was soon to be the top-scoring squadron in Britain's Desert Air Force.

## Abyssinia

In March 1941, General Wavell launched his last offensive, against the Italian Empire in Abyssinia, which for nine months had been cut off from supplies. His Indian and South African columns moved quickly across the country, and entered Addis Ababa in April and restored the Emperor Haile Selassie to his throne. Wavell had now fought six consecutive campaigns – Libya, Greece, Iraq, Crete, Syria and Abyssinia.

## Attempt to relieve Tobruk

In June 1941, Wavell mounted his seventh campaign – an attempt to break through to Tobruk. But the British lost 100 tanks and Tobruk was left to fight on through the summer heat. Churchill was convinced that Wavell was a tired man. On 22 June, Wavell was transferred to the post of C-in-C in India, and was replaced by General Claude Auchinleck, a younger man.

## Enigma and Ultra: codebreaking

Churchill had received warning of the German attack on Crete through an amazing breakthrough – British codebreakers had managed to 'crack' the workings of the code machine used to send wireless messages by Germany's armed forces. Known as 'Enigma', the Germans' code machine was a form of typewriter with revolving drums bearing letters and was capable of millions of settings. However, Britain's mathematical geniuses built the world's first computer to process the German data they intercepted. Its decoded messages – 'Ultra' – gave Britain some warning of enemy intentions, and remained the best-kept secret of the war.

# *1941*: Hitler invades Russia

**A**t dawn on 22 June 1941, Hitler's armies began 'Operation Barbarossa' – their attack on Soviet Russia. Hitler launched the most powerful army ever assembled – 160 divisions supported by 2,600 aircraft along the entire 2,000-kilometre front, from Leningrad in the north (where 12 Finnish divisions joined the Germans) to the south, where 11 Romanian divisions also advanced on Odessa as allies of Germany.

Three immense army groups spearheaded by tank divisions struck deep into Russia and broke the enemy front with ease. Hitler had assured his generals: *'We will only have to kick down the door and the whole rotten structure will come crashing down'*. Once more, he seemed right. In the Baltic states and the Ukraine, German forces were welcomed as liberators, and one million Russians became prisoners in the first week. Behind the German Army came the SS and Gestapo Death Squads, murdering thousands of Jews and Communist Commissars without mercy. The Russian campaign would be a war of annihilation.

**Below: In September 1941 most of the Australians in Tobruk were relieved by fresh British troops, but when the siege ended in December there were still some Australians left to clown for the cameras.**

On hearing of the German invasion, Churchill broadcast that he would give all available aid to Russia. This shocked the many British people who viewed Stalin and Communism as evil and oppressive. By late July 1941, the German tanks were approaching Moscow, but Hitler, to the despair of his field marshals, ordered the offensives switched to the south to envelop the Russian armies defending Smolensk and Kiev (which fell along with 600,000 Russians). In October, when even the Crimea (except Sevastopol) had fallen to the Germans, Hitler's armies resumed their push on Moscow, but the snow was already falling and soon the roads turned to mud. Close to 1.5 million Russians had become prisoners.

On 2 December 1941, the Germans reached the outskirts of Moscow and caught sight of the towers of the Kremlin. Two days later, the Russian armies under General Zhukov counter-attacked with a ferocity and strength the enemy had not expected. Stalin had withdrawn his last reserves – his army in Siberia – and committed it to battle. The Germans were driven back. Moscow was never again threatened. Leningrad was to undergo a 900-day siege, but by Christmas 1941 the German armies freezing in the winter snows had suffered 750,000 casualties. Hitler had hoped to crush Russia's armies in six months.

Russia's vast expanses were its asset and the Russians would prove unconquerable. Hitler had gambled and lost.

## Increasing American aid

In 1940, America's President Roosevelt had given Britain 50 old destroyers in return for leases on West Indies naval bases, and had introduced conscription. But following his great election victory later in November 1940, Roosevelt went further in helping Britain. In March 1941, the American Congress passed the 'Lend-Lease' Bill – in effect 'lending' Britain armaments, aircraft and seven billion dollars.

In August 1941, Roosevelt and Churchill met for the first time and struck up a rare partnership. They pledged in the 'Atlantic Charter' to work together until 'the final destruction of the Nazi tyranny' – these were fighting words from a neutral nation. More importantly, the US Navy undertook to patrol the western Atlantic and escort convoys against German U-boat attack.

## Disasters, November 1941: Tobruk relieved

By September 1941, when all enemy attempts to capture Tobruk had failed, most of the weary Australian defenders were relieved by fresh British troops. On 18 November, the new British C-in-C, General Auchinleck, launched his desert

Above: Germany's war against Russia was fought from its first days as a war of total destruction.

force – now named 8th Army – to relieve Tobruk and destroy Rommel's German-Italian Army. Within four days, most of his 500 tanks were immobilised by mechanical failure or destroyed by the Afrika Korps' superior tanks, artillery and tactics. But the New Zealand Division, despite suffering 5,000 casualties, had already pressed on to Tobruk, and they made contact with it on 7 December 1941. Rommel's battered army retreated towards Tripoli.

November 1941 saw the British Fleet in the Mediterranean suffer enormous losses – HMAS *Parramatta* was sunk (only 24 of her 160 sailors survived), the Italians sank two battleships in Alexandria Harbour, German U-boats sank the *Barham* and the carrier *Ark Royal*.

## HMAS *Sydney* lost

A tragedy occurred closer to home. During 1941, as Japan's intentions became of great concern to Australia, HMAS *Sydney*, veteran of many Mediterranean battles, was retained in Australian waters. *Sydney* was off the Western Australian coast on 19 November 1941 when she sighted a suspicious merchant ship and drew closer to investigate it. The mysterious ship was the disguised German raider *Kormoran*, which opened fire at point-blank range. *Sydney* was mortally wounded but succeeded in setting *Kormoran* on fire before drifting away, wracked by explosions. Nothing was ever found of *Sydney* or her 645 officers and men.

### AUSSIES

AFTER CRETE DISASTER ANZAC TROOPS ARE NOW BEING RUTHLESSLY SACRIFICED BY ENGLAND IN TOBRUCH AND SYRIA.

TURKEY HAS CONCLUDED PACT OF FRIENDSHIP WITH GERMANY. ENGLAND WILL SHORTLY BE DRIVEN OUT OF THE MEDITERRANEAN. OFFENSIVE FROM EGYPT TO RELIEVE YOU TOTALLY SMASHED.

YOU CANNOT ESCAPE.

OUR DIVE BOMBERS ARE WAITING TO SINK YOUR TRANSPORTS. THINK OF YOUR FUTURE AND YOUR PEOPLE AT HOME.

COME FORWARD - SHOW WHITE FLAGS AND YOU WILL BE OUT OF DANGER !

### SURRENDER !!

Above: During the siege in Tobruk, the Nazis dropped leaflets to try and convince the Australians that they were being sacrificed.

# 1941: Japan strikes in the Pacific

## Japan's march to war

During 1941, Japan's aggressive moves had increased. In July 1941, the Japanese entered southern Indo-China. When President Roosevelt placed a stoppage on America's oil and metal exports to Japan, the militarist group in Tokyo stated that Japan would die of economic strangulation. In October 1941, the extremist General Tojo became Japan's prime minister and plans were made for a sudden conquest of the British, Dutch and American possessions in South-East Asia. The oil of the Dutch East Indies and Borneo, the tin and rubber of Malaya, and the rice of Burma and the Philippines would form part of the new Japanese empire – the 'Greater East-Asia Co-Prosperity Sphere'.

The British regarded Japan as a second-rate country, with a poor army and unlikely to risk war with Britain and the United States. They were gravely in error. Admiral Yamamoto assured Tojo that he could eliminate the American fleet and that conquering the undefended South-East Asia would be 'child's play' – but a negotiated peace

**General Tojo, leader of the extremists in Japan, became prime minister in October 1941 and led Japan into war.**

would have to be sought, or America's power would eventually overwhelm Japan. On the morning of Sunday 7 December 1941, planes from Japanese aircraft carriers attacked the US Pacific Fleet at its anchorage in Pearl Harbor in Hawaii, and sank four battleships. Japan's principal objective, the US Fleet's three aircraft carriers, were not in Pearl Harbor and thus missed destruction.

## Defeat in Malaya and Singapore

While Japanese aircraft were attacking Pearl Harbor, other Japanese attacks were falling on the north-east coast of Malaya and on American bases on Wake Island, Midway Island, the Philippines, and the British colony of Hong Kong. America's President Roosevelt asked Congress for an immediate declaration of war; Germany then declared war on the United States. The European war had become the Second World War.

Churchill left for the United States to forge with Roosevelt a 'Grand Alliance' to destroy Nazi Germany. In the Pacific, the Allies would fight a holding war until victory was achieved in Europe.

In response to Australia's increasing demands that Britain reinforce Singapore, Churchill had sent out the battleship *Prince of Wales* and the battle-cruiser *Repulse*. Both great ships were sunk off the Malay coast by Japanese torpedo-bombers on the second day of war. Since the 1920s, Australia and New Zealand had depended on a British fleet at the great naval base of Singapore, but when war came the fleet was non-existent. The British described Singapore as an 'impregnable fortress' – but it was almost defenceless. Instead of the 556 modern aircraft considered necessary to defend it, there were only 161, all of them obsolete. The Australian squadrons were flying slow 'Buffalo' fighters that were no match for the extraordinarily fast enemy 'Zero'. The British had not imagined the Japanese approaching Singapore from the north, through Malaya.

Malaya was defended by only two ill-trained Indian divisions and, in the south, by the 8th Australian Division, but the troops had no tanks, no strong defence lines. The Japanese struck inland and then south, forcing the British to evacuate their airfields, and bypassed the British roadblocks. The campaign was fought in monsoonal rain and a humidity that sapped the defender's strength and morale. By Christmas Day 1941, after only two weeks, the Indian forces had retreated to Ipoh and had lost a third of Malaya.

# Australia looks to America

Christmas 1941 was the most anxious in Australia's memory. Australia's four trained divisions (6th, 7th, 8th and 9th) were all overseas, her air defence threadbare. On 27 December, Australia's Prime Minister John Curtin released to the press an historic statement:

'We refuse to accept the dictum that the Pacific struggle must be treated as a subordinate segment of the general conflict. Without any inhibitions of any kind, I make it quite clear that Australia looks to America, free of any pangs as to our traditional links or kinship with the United Kingdom.'

## Malaya and Singapore fall

All of Malaya had been lost by mid-January 1942 when General Percival committed his best troops, the 8th Australian Division, to battle. The Australians ambushed enemy columns and counter-attacked vigorously, but within a fortnight Percival ordered a retreat to Singapore Island. The new Supreme Commander, General Wavell, ordered Singapore to be defended to the last round. On 9 February 1941, the Japanese crossed the narrow strait from Johore and pushed inland. By now, Singapore was crowded with close to a million people and under heavy bombing. Reinforcements were shipped to Singapore, but they arrived just in time to be captured.

The British retreated to a ring around Singapore city in the south. Counter-attacks proved fruitless. The water supply was cut. On 15 February 1941, Percival asked for a cease-fire. The Japanese demanded complete surrender. The Japanese, with an army of only 35,000 men, took the surrender of an army of 130,000 Indian, British, Australian and Malay troops. Churchill called the fall of Singapore the 'greatest disaster to British arms which our history affords'.

In October 1941, John Curtin, leader of the Australian Labor Party, became prime minister. Curtin led Australia until the eve of victory in 1945.

# 1942: Defeat in the east

## The islands fall

The Japanese tide swept south, swamping everything in its path. The small Australian **garrisons** at Rabaul on New Britain and on Ambon were overwhelmed; hundreds of Australian soldiers were massacred. On 19 February 1942, Japanese aircraft mounted a sudden attack on Darwin, sinking six ships and leaving more than 500 killed and wounded. It was the first time enemy bombs had fallen on Australian soil, and not the last.

## Java

On the day Singapore fell, the first ships carrying the 7th Australian Division, returning from the Middle East, landed in Java. Churchill had diverted their convoy towards Burma, which was collapsing under Japanese attack, but Prime Minister Curtin angrily ordered it back on its course for Java. The 6th Division following in its wake was diverted on urgent request of the British to Ceylon, where it was kept until July. Curtin agreed that the 9th Division should remain in the Middle East. Australia's three remaining veteran AIF troops were overseas when the Japanese threatened their homeland.

On 27 February 1942, aircraft reported that the Japanese were approaching Java, and the American,

**General Douglas MacArthur led US and Australian forces in the South-West Pacific to victory against the Japanese in 1945.**

British, Dutch and Australian (ABDA) naval force sailed out to destroy them, only to be sunk in the Battle of the Java Sea. On the next day, Australia's surviving cruiser HMAS *Perth*, accompanied by USS *Houston*, was ordered to make for home waters. But on the night of 28 February, the cruisers struck the western enemy fleet of 64 ships in Sunda Strait, and they were both sunk after a famous night battle.

On Java, the under-equipped Dutch-Indonesian force and the Australian brigade fought on until 2 March 1942. Only four days later, the Japanese entered Rangoon. In the Philippines, the Americans were holding out on Corrigedor Island in Manila Bay. (They were forced to surrender on 5 May 1942.)

Japan had conquered South-East Asia in just three months. The only forces still fighting behind enemy lines were several hundred Australian commandos in the mountains of East Timor.

## Prisoners of war

For Australia, the war with Japan was a traumatic episode that left enduring bitterness. The sufferings of the 22,000 Australian soldiers captured in the disasters of 1942 were terrible: 35 per cent of them – more than 8,000 – died in captivity of starvation, disease and brutality, and their sufferings on the Burma-Thailand railway became a byword for despair. Only 242 of the 7,000 captured Australians died in German prison camps.

## Pacific victories: Coral Sea and Midway

In this dark period of unrelenting defeat, the Japanese met with two unexpected setbacks. Attempting to seize the great harbour of Port

Moresby on New Guinea's south-east coast, two Japanese fleets steamed for the port, but the Americans had cracked the enemy naval code. They positioned their aircraft carriers in the Coral Sea to intercept them, supported by the Australian cruisers *Australia*, *Canberra* and *Hobart*. In a confused action over 7–8 May 1942, American carrier planes sank or damaged three carriers for the loss of one of their own. The Japanese never again threatened Moresby by sea, and just a month later they suffered an even greater defeat. In attempting to seize Midway Island in the north Pacific, the Japanese lost three aircraft carriers in succession (4 June 1942).

Japan scrapped plans for further advances. She would now have to fight to defend her conquests against an American fleet growing in strength.

## The Battle of the Atlantic

The war at sea covered the oceans of the globe and much of it was fought underwater. German submarines (or U-boats) threatened Allied survival. By early 1942, losses of merchant ships were mounting. The British Arctic convoys to Russia also faced a threat from German aircraft and warships stationed in Norway. Churchill declared that 'The Battle of the Atlantic' must be won. Escort warships braved the winter seas of the North Atlantic equipped with asdic (a form of radar) to locate submerged submarines, and lethal 'depth charges' that exploded underwater, crushing U-boats' hulls.

After six months of constant defeat, American and Australian naval forces struck back at the Japanese and won a victory in the Battle of the Coral Sea in May 1942.

As submarines had to spend most of their time on the surface, Coastal Command flew on constant patrol, often sighting and attacking their prey before they could dive. But the U-boats sank more than 2,800 ships and took the lives of nearly 50,000 Allied seamen before the tide turned late in 1943. More than 700 U-boats were sunk and with them 28,000 German crewmen. After mid-1943, convoys carrying food, troops, tanks and munitions were able to cross from America to Britain with relative safety.

# MacArthur and the Americans

Late in March 1942, General Douglas MacArthur, the commander of the US and Filipino forces in the Philippines, was ordered to make his way to Australia to become 'Supreme Allied Commander, South-West Pacific'. MacArthur, the image of a hero, quickly established a close relationship with Prime Minister Curtin, and made his headquarters in Brisbane. The first American counter-offensive came in August 1942, when US Marines landed on Guadalcanal, in the southern Solomons, which was the scene of fighting that lasted six months.

# 1942: Turning the tide

## The Kokoda campaign

**B**ut the most dramatic campaign began when the Japanese troops landed on the north-east coast of Papua New Guinea in July 1942. Having failed to seize Moresby by sea, they would approach Port Moresby overland, crossing the high Owen Stanley Ranges on a narrow 'track' leading from Kokoda village. The trek would take them seven days over rugged mountains, through leech-infested rainforest, across torrential rivers.

The only troops in Kokoda were a battalion of young Australian militia, the 39th Battalion, who fought desperately from 23 July to 7 August 1942 to defend the village. As the enemy force grew to 5,000 men, the Australians made a fighting retreat. On 23 August, the exhausted young militiamen were joined by the battalions of desert veterans of the 7th Division at Isurava. The Japanese expected an unopposed 'seven day'

march, but after four weeks of fighting were barely halfway across the mountains: a tribute to the remarkable bravery of the young Australian soldiers. But the Australians were forced to fall back, closely pursued by the Japanese. The retreat was a nightmare: past the torrent of Eora Creek, up to the grassy clearing of Myola (where tree-hopping Allied aircraft dropped them supplies), then back to Efogi village, with the Papuan natives ('The Fuzzy-Wuzzy Angels') carrying their wounded. By 17 September 1942, the Australians had fallen back to the last ridge before Moresby: Imita Ridge. There they would make a last stand.

But the Japanese were now exhausted after two months of grim fighting, half-starving and demoralised. On 26 September, the Australians moved forward to find the Japanese had with-drawn. The Australian advance now became a pursuit and the enemy was hunted mercilessly. The grim counter-offensive continued until 3 November when the Australians recaptured Kokoda village and raised the Australian flag.

## Milne Bay

Meanwhile, the Japanese had made a second landing to threaten Port Moresby. On 25 August 1942, they landed troops on the eastern tip of Papua New Guinea to secure the fine harbour of Milne Bay. Australian troops counter-attacked and the seesaw battle raged amid the mangrove swamps and muddy foreshores until 6 September, when the Japanese survivors were evacuated. At Milne Bay and Kokoda, Australians had become the first troops to outfight the Japanese.

**Australian soldiers guarding three Japanese prisoners at Gona-Buna in 1943.**

# Desert victory: Alamein

In the Middle East and in Russia, the summer of 1942 had been a time of crisis – it looked as if the Axis powers were within grasp of victory. In June 1942, a massive German offensive was launched that soon carried its armies as far as the Volga and the great industrial city of Stalingrad, and into the Caucasus and the Grozny oilfields on the very borders of Asia.

In January 1942, Rommel again attacked in Libya. By February, the 8th Army had retreated 500 kilometres and was attempting to establish a new defence line. Malta was almost starving, subjected to ceaseless bombing and seemed about to fall. On 21 June, Rommel captured Tobruk, defended by the 2nd South African Division, and pushed on towards Cairo. In late June, the 9th Australian Division – 'The Rats of Tobruk' – and New Zealanders were ordered south from Syria to defend Egypt once more.

During July 1942, the battered 8th Army held a line running south from El Alamein against constant Axis attacks. The Australians counter-attacked constantly in July, driving back the enemy, who were now exhausted and had out-run their supplies and fuel. In August, Churchill himself arrived in Cairo. He sacked Auchinleck and replaced him as C-in-C Middle East with General Sir Harold Alexander, a youthful front-line general. He chose an obscure lieutenant-general called Bernard Montgomery to command the 8th Army.

Montgomery galvanized the 8th Army. He ordered the army to fight where it stood. When Rommel attacked 18 days later, the 8th Army was dug-in and ready, and repelled the attack. Montgomery built up his army and launched his own offensive on the night of 23 October 1942, after a massive artillery barrage. But 8th Army failed to fight their way through minefields one-kilometre deep. On day two, Montgomery asked the 9th Australian Division in the far north to carry the weight of the battle and continue their attacks. This they did until 2 November, when Montgomery launched his breakthrough offensive in the south with armour and broke the enemy line, plunging Rommel's army into headlong retreat. Alamein was the last great battle fought by the Australians in Egypt, and perhaps their greatest victory. They had lost 5,000 men since July.

On 8 November 1942, Anglo-American armies under the command of General Dwight Eisenhower landed in north-west Africa at the other end of the Mediterranean. Caught between two advancing Allied armies, Rommel retreated into the mountains of Tunisia.

The Australian soldiers returning from the Middle East were greeted as heroes by their families.

# 1943: The 'soft underbelly': Allied offensives

In January 1943, as the Allied armies were entering Tunisia, it was clear that a turning point in the war had been reached and that the Allies had the initiative. Churchill and Roosevelt met at Casablanca in Morocco to plan the next steps in their strategy. They decided to attack Europe's 'soft underbelly' – Sicily and Italy. They would intensify the bombing of Germany and accept nothing but the 'unconditional surrender' of Germany.

Meanwhile, the Russian ring was tightening on Stalingrad. On 2 February 1943, the remnants of the German 6th Army surrendered. Of the 330,000 German troops who had been encircled, only 90,000 were left to surrender. It was the greatest defeat in military history.

The Allies were defeating the Japanese in the Pacific. In January 1943, the Japanese retreating from Kokoda were finally destroyed in their bunkers on the coast at Gona and Buna by Australian and American troops. In February, when Guadalcanal was secured, the southern approaches of the Solomon Islands were cleared, providing an avenue for an Allied approach to northern New Guinea and the Philippines. In September 1943, the 9th Division landed in the Huon Gulf of New Guinea to eradicate the Japanese garrisons there, while other forces pushed up from the south. The Australian advance continued over the mountains to the northern coast. It was the active end of the role of the Australian Army for a year, though the navy and a growing air force remained in the forefront of MacArthur's westward advance, bypassing Japanese garrisons.

## Kursk

In July 1943, as the Allied armies invaded Sicily, the Germans attempted to remove the great Russian **salient** at Kursk. It proved to be the greatest tank-battle in history, involving 5,000 tanks. The German offensive was crushed by the Russians, who were well dug-in with artillery and anti-tank guns. After a week, the Germans gave up, having lost more than 2,000 tanks and 70,000 men. Russian losses were also heavy, but the Germans were never again strong enough to mount an offensive. From Kursk onward, the Russian armies were on the offensive.

**In the Pacific, Australian airmen flew American fighters such as these Kittyhawks against the Japanese. In these aircraft, the airmen were spared the terrible losses of the bomber aircrews.**

## Sicily and the fall of Mussolini

On 10 July 1943, the victorious Allied armies moved from Tunisia and landed in Sicily. The Italian troops were weary after three years of war and were quick to surrender, especially after Mussolini was removed from power by King Victor Emmanuel on 25 July. On 3 September, the Allies landed in Italy.

## The air force

Air power used in land battles – dive-bombers, fighter aircraft – had proved effective, but expectations that bombers could be the 'strategic' weapon that would bring a speedy end to the war itself had been proved wrong. In nearly three years of war, British bombers in constant night-raids destroyed less than five per cent of Germany's industry. The aircraft were too light to carry heavy bomb loads and lacked precision bombing aids. Losses of British bombers to enemy fighters and anti-aircraft fire were so heavy that historians have claimed that the bombing campaign had set back Britain's war effort more than it did Germany's.

In mid-1942 things began to change when Britain began mounting 'Thousand Bomber' night-raids on German cities. A brilliant young Australian, Don Bennett, formed a 'Path Finder' force to fly ahead of the bombers and drop flares to identify the targets. The giant four-engine Avro Lancaster heavy bomber went into service, and by 1943 was the mainstay of Bomber Command. The trained aircrew from the EATS scheme now provided the

**Australian bomber aircrew in Europe suffered heavy losses during the bombing offensives against Germany in 1942–45.**

crews for the bombers – by war's end young men from the Dominions provided 40 per cent of all aircrew in the British air force (RAF). Most served in RAF squadrons. The exploits of the eight Australian squadrons scattered through Bomber Command became legendary.

In 1943, the Allied air forces were ordered to carry out *'the progressive destruction and dislocation of the German military, industrial and economic system, and the undermining of the morale of the German people to a point where their capacity for armed resistance is fatally weakened.'* The RAF flew at night, the American 8th Air Force's B-17s (Flying Fortresses) flew by day, hitting German cities and industrial centres. Hamburg, Cologne, Dusseldorff, Berlin and Nuremburg were hammered. By war's end, the bomber had become the Allies' most effective weapon of destruction, leaving Germany in ruins, clearing the way for the armies.

# The bombing campaign

The bombing campaign caused more controversy than any other aspect of Allied strategy. It caused enormous civilian casualties (perhaps 600,000 German civilians died) and fatalities among aircrew were heavy. Its supporters state that the Allies were fighting a ruthless enemy whose entire record was a crime against humanity. The aircrew had little opinion either way. They simply did their duty, at great risk, living with death on every mission. Often 10 per cent of the bomber force was lost. More than 170,000 young Allied aircrew died in the air war. Marshal Kesselring of the *Luftwaffe* was to confess that 'Allied air power was the greatest single reason for the German defeat'.

# 1944: Closing in

During 1944, the Allies carried out the most dramatic advances of the war. In May 1944, as the worst of the winter mud dried, General Alexander's armies in Italy broke through the Monte Cassino line and on 5 June entered Rome. One day later, the long-awaited Allied invasion of France began.

## Normandy: D-Day

At dawn on 6 June 1944, the greatest armada of ships the world had ever seen landed General Eisenhower's British, American and Canadian forces on the beaches of Normandy. Initial casualties were light because the invasion had been planned brilliantly and Allied Intelligence had led the Germans to believe that the main invasion would fall further north near Calais. But the Battle for Normandy grew in intensity, lasting a month before General Patton's tanks broke out of the bridgehead from the west.

From August 1944, the German armies were in chaotic retreat, hammered by the Allied air forces. The Allies liberated Paris on 25 August, Brussels one week later, and hoped to end the war by Christmas. But the airborne attempt to capture the Rhine bridges at Arnhem failed, the Germans counter-attacked in Belgium, and winter snows froze all operations. Hitler hurled his 'secret weapon' – rockets – against London, but most of his 10,000 V-1 flying bombs were destroyed before they struck the city.

## The Eastern Front

In late June 1944, the Russian armies launched their massive summer offensive, and poured into eastern Europe. By late July, the Red Army had reached the outskirts of Warsaw; by late August they had entered Romania and by September they invaded Bulgaria, forcing the Germans to evacuate Greece and retreat through Yugoslavia.

American infantrymen make their way through the ruins of a French town.

## The Pacific

With most of her armies stalemated in China, Japan now faced the US Navy's Task Forces crossing the central Pacific, where the Marine Corps – protected by powerful carriers and battleships – stormed island after island. Japan's dwindling air force was destroyed. In the Marianas in June 1944, American fliers shot down 346 enemy aircraft for the loss of only 40 of their own.

In the south-west Pacific, MacArthur continued to leapfrog along the northern coast of New Guinea, seizing Morotai in September (it became the base for the RAAF's strong 1st Tactical Air Force). In October 1944, MacArthur fulfiled his promise to return to the Philippines, landing boldly at Leyte in October 1944. The Japanese attempted to destroy the fleet, but the great naval Battle of Leyte Gulf was an American – and Australian – victory against the Japanese. Late in 1944, Australian troops entered Bougainville, New Britain, and northern New Guinea to 'clear out' the bypassed Japanese garrisons.

## The Axis crumbles

As the Allied armies pushed into Nazi-occupied Europe, they discovered evidence of mass murder and brutality that shocked the world. In January 1945, the Red Army found at Auschwitz a vast extermination camp. Hitler's Europe had been built on terror and genocide. Millions of Russian prisoners and people from eastern Europe were worked as slaves until they died.

As early as May 1939 Hitler had vowed in the Reichstag that '*if the international Jewish financiers … should again succeed in plunging Europe into a world war the result will be … the extermination of the Jewish race throughout Europe.*' It is not known why Hitler had such homicidal hatred for Jews. Orthodox Jews comprised barely one per cent of Germany's population, and they were among the most successful and patriotic of Germany's citizens. Hitler deprived them of civil rights in 1935,

and his fanatical Nazi units drawn from Himmler's SS after 1939 confined Europe's Jewish communities to ghettos or camps, where they died rapidly of starvation, disease and mass shootings.

## The Holocaust

Early in January 1942, the Nazi leaders decided to go one step further. Shootings 'upset' Himmler's Death Squads, and he viewed bullets as slow and inefficient. The Nazis resolved to exterminate the Jewish people by poison gas, and to burn their bodies in crematoria. Across Poland vast death camps were built – Auschwitz, Maidenek, Treblinka among them. Each was to dispose of more than a million Jews. Defenceless Jewish men, women and children waited in terror for orders to assemble with their belongings for 'resettlement' in eastern Europe, not knowing the fate that awaited them.

By 1945, more than six million of Europe's eight million Jews had been murdered. The Jews call the crime the Holocaust. Allied tribunals later sentenced several hundred Nazi officers and officials to death or prison for crimes against humanity.

The Holocaust is a nightmare that still haunts the world.

## Resistance

The bravest of Europe's peoples sought to resist Nazi rule. They were a minority because most people simply sought to survive enemy Occupation. But after 1942, resistance movements grew in number, and were supplied by British Intelligence and Special Operations, who parachuted them arms, radio transmitters, codes and liaison officers. All resisters faced torture and death from the Nazi Gestapo if captured. Their stories are among the most heroic of the war.

# 1945: The defeat of Germany and Japan

By early 1945, it was clear that Germany and Japan were doomed, but no one could predict how much longer the war would last. To gain bases close to Japan, the American fleet landed Marines on Iwo Jima in February 1945; the 25,000 Japanese there fought to the death and inflicted 26,000 casualties on the Americans. In April 1945, the Americans landed on Okinawa and suffered 50,000 killed and wounded, and Australian forces landed in Borneo in June. In April, President Roosevelt died of a massive heart attack, worn out by the strain of war.

In February 1945, with the defeat of Germany only three months away, the 'Big Three' – Churchill, Roosevelt and Stalin – met at Yalta to plan the post-war world. Within months of final victory, the great wartime alliance of the West and the Soviet Union had crumbled and the Cold War had begun.

## Germany surrenders

In January 1945, the Russian armies poured into east Prussia; millions of German civilians fled but few escaped. In March, the American, British and French armies crossed the Rhine and struck deeply into Germany. On 25 April, the American and Russian armies met at Torgau on the Elbe. Germany was now cut in two. Its armies in Austria, Czechoslovakia, northern Yugoslavia and Hungary were left to the oncoming Russians. The Russians then closed the ring around Berlin.

Hitler, by now a nervous wreck kept functioning by drugs, remained in Berlin in the bunker beneath his shattered Reich Chancellery. On 29 April 1945, he heard that Mussolini had been captured by Italian partisans and shot. On 30 April 1945, as Russian tanks approached his underground bunker, Hitler took poison and shot himself. His body was burned in a ditch; a fitting fate.

On 5 May 1945, the German armies in north-west Europe surrendered to Field-Marshal Montgomery. The unconditional surrender of all German armed forces was signed at General Eisenhower's headquarters on 7 May. On the following day, Churchill proclaimed Victory in Europe. VE-Day was celebrated throughout the world with an explosion of natural joy never before known in history. The nightmare was nearly over.

## The fall of Japan

Only Japan remained to be defeated. As MacArthur and Admiral Nimitz planned the invasion of Japan, warning President Truman that it could cost a million Allied casualties, the

American president asked Japan to surrender or face the consequences. Reluctantly, he decided to use a terrifying new weapon – the atomic bomb, so powerful that it could destroy an entire city.

On 6 August 1945, an American Super Fortress dropped an atomic bomb on Hiroshima; it killed 64,000 Japanese in seconds. Three days later, a second atomic bomb was dropped on Nagasaki. Japan surrendered on 14 August. On 2 September 1945, Japan signed the surrender on the deck of the battleship USS *Missouri* in Tokyo Bay. The Second World War was over.

## The Allied victory

Britain and the Dominions had bravely fought alone for a year in 1940–41. But American war production and Russian manpower won the war. By war's end in 1945, the United States alone had produced 300,000 military aircraft, 90,000 tanks, 71,000 naval ships (including 100 aircraft carriers), three million machine-guns, and had raised armed forces totalling 15 million men. The cost was staggering – more than $250,000 million, a debt that had to be handed on to succeeding generations to pay. Given a choice between defeat or debt, the Allies chose the latter.

Despite Russia's loss of five million men as prisoners (only two million survived German captivity), her army also suffered four million killed in battle; another 13 million Soviet civilians (including nearly two million Jews) died of starvation, epidemics or mass murder. Nearly 90 per cent of German fatalities occurred on the Eastern Front. Without Russia's sacrifice, Allied victory would have been impossible.

Britain suffered the loss of 400,000 dead, America 250,000. Nations that had entered the war lightly suffered horrifically: German dead were seven million (half of them civilians); Japan lost two million; Italy 400,000.

Australia mourned nearly 30,000 dead (8,000 of whom died in Japanese captivity) and New Zealand 10,000. These losses seem small in

relation to the death toll of the war; even Australia's production of only 1,200 aircraft seems insignificant. Strategically, however, Australia was indispensable as the main base for the war against Japan, and her famous fighting men played a decisive role whenever they entered battle, from Libya to Kokoda and Alamein.

The Second World War showed the strength of democracy. The political leaders such as Churchill and Roosevelt enjoyed near-dictatorial powers, but unlike Hitler they never overruled the strategic advice of their military chiefs. Their soldiers had confidence in their front-line generals, who took care to minimize casualties. Eisenhower ('Ike'), Montgomery ('Monty'), Alexander ('Alex') and MacArthur were all household names and became popular heroes. The people were subjected to numerous wartime laws and restrictions, but their basic freedoms were not suspended. The people had confidence in their leaders – Churchill, Roosevelt and Curtin – who were inspiring figures who forged rare partnerships.

After victory in 1945, the Allies put the Nazi leaders on trial for 'crimes against humanity', but they neither victimised nor terrorised the defeated nations. Instead, they used their resources to rebuild Germany and Japan's shattered societies and self-respect – to make 'a kinder world'. This was the Second World War's greatest victory.

**When Japan surrendered, Australian troops were still fighting isolated pockets of the enemy in the South-West Pacific.**

# Glossary

| | |
|---|---|
| armistice | cease-fire |
| blitzkrieg | 'lightning war': sudden overwhelming attack by tanks, bombers and ground troops |
| coalition | government formed by a combination of parties |
| Communist | originally Bolshevik – a political party committed to the overthrow of capitalist and democratic societies |
| conscription | compulsory military service |
| dictatorship | rule by one leader |
| disarmament | reduction in weapons |
| Dominions | self-governing nations of the British Empire, such as Australia |
| garrison | army base or fortress |
| Great Powers | major nations of Europe |
| munitions | shells, bullets and bombs |
| neutrality | uncommitted to war on any side |
| propaganda | government-controlled media |
| recession | economic downturn |
| Reich | German 'realm' or Empire |
| Reichstag | German parliament |
| salient | bulge in front line |
| stalemate | deadlock |

# Index